PURSUIT OF WEALTH

WEALTH CREATION STRATEGIES

MALLIKARJUNA SASALWAD
MUDDUGALMATH

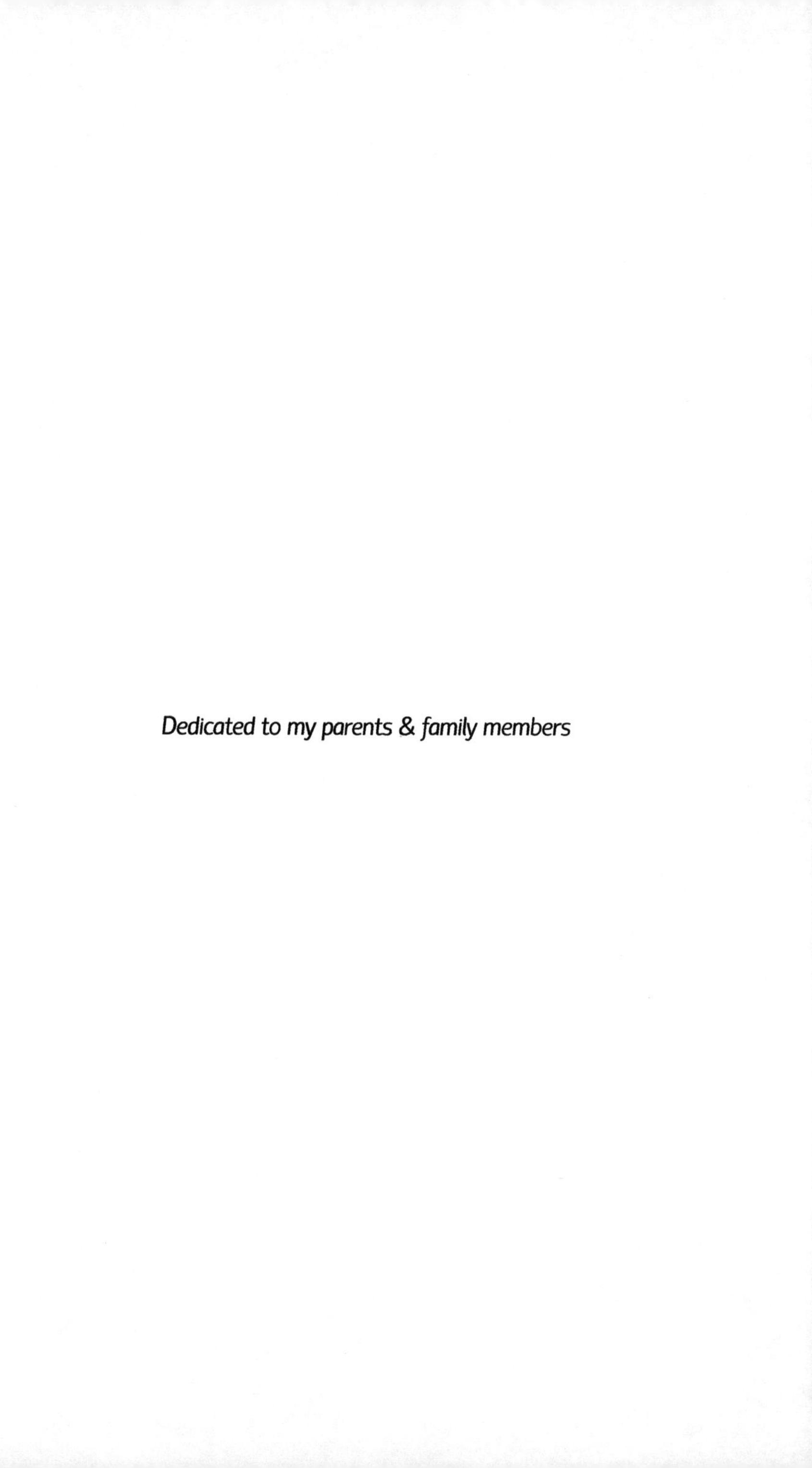

Dedicated to my parents & family members

Contents

Preface

We have People with specific skills who can create wealth in a matter of no time. What are tools, techniques, and skills they have figured out that a normal person has yet to find out? Some people are struggling to feed their families even post putting a lot of effort, heart, and soul into what they are doing. Few others, earn millions sitting at home and enjoying vacation with family.

Pursuit of Wealth is an eye-opener book that reveals secrets, experiences, and strategies proven by some leading entrepreneurs. If one truly seeking wealth should turn around and look altogether at a new dimension of the world. This book will get you useful insights and guidance to strategize your wealth creation plan

Acknowledgements

To my parent who guided me in all aspects of life, to my spouse and kids who have been inspirational in my activities, and to family members & friends.

Prologue

Right from my early school days, I have had a habit of collecting. Collection of chocolate wrappers, cards of colors, stickers, photos, and old coins. As a grown-up, this habit changed into a different dimension of habits. Likewise, in my early 20s, had a passion for riding bikes, and cars, traveling around new places with friends, and making lots of new friends. I would say this is more of an experiences collection rather than a materialistic aspect the collection.

Similarly, as I grew up until my early 40 this changed into reading books, managing, and learning new skills apart from my regular day job. Some of which include how to effectively manage personal finances, spending frugally, fundamental wealth creation principles, and so on.

In search of the same, I was trying to figure out how a genuine "Wealth", not "Money" is created. What it takes for a normal average person like you and me to do it. How you can get really rich by even in your holidays and while you are sleeping on any part of the earth.

The more I went on digging and searching for my questions, the more I got answers. Not a single answer but a practically infinite number of answers. But at the core, what are the principles of wealth creation techniques and principles.

These principles are found by a few leaders and creative people out there in the world. They saw everything from a different microscopic angle, creative angle, and philosophical angle.

Built, redefined, altered, formed a core team then eventually became a success.

This book tries to find answers for mine and as well yours revolving around many years unanswered. If you are also one of me, then please do reach out and share with your loved ones, I am sure you will love the insights.

CHAPTER ONE

Philosophy

Even though the word "Philosophy" seems to be a little old-fashioned but it is one of the most important parts of any wealth creation process. If you are an average person with a 9-5 kind of job or you own a small piece of business or something else, but if you want to redefine the process of wealth creation, you should have some principles, some philosophy laid out even before you start to plan and execute it.

Let me take an example of one of India's Fintech "Zerodha". The company has generated millions of revenue with practically zero cost. The success story behind Zerodha is truly philosophical. The founder Nitin Kamath has formed and stuck to that philosophy way years before. Even before the company was born in the first place.

When a lot of people asked this question for Nithin Kamath, how is Zerodha profitable when most of the new-age companies aren't? The simple answer he gave was "Their cost of acquisition was zero". If they had to spend heavily on acquiring resources and people, they wouldn't be"

The cost of acquisition was a decision they made philosophical. When a lot of new-age tech companies spent millions and billions of dollars in acquiring user bases and technology platforms. These fellows spent "Zero" in both building platforms and creating a large user base.

. If they had to provide a quality system, quality values at literally lesser than their rival companies, then you have to think of an altogether new angle, new dimension, a new direction, isn't it? You would need a new compass to take you to a new destination.

Image of Philosophy: Try and identify what you see from your view.

CHAPTER TWO

Pillars of Wealth

For an oak tree to grow 100 meters high in the sky, it can't stand still when the stormy wind or rain comes if it just leaves its roots on the surface of the ground or by just clinging its branches to side rocks. The roots should go as deep as beyond, even the tallest branch of its own reaches the sky. So is our health. Health should be deep-rooted to stand still any small big Tsunami of illness should come and go without any effect to it.

If you work day and night for a day or two and fall sick for the next 4 days means, it is as good as not working or far less than working 8 hours a day. Keeping the physical body fit all the time is the first and foremost important part.

Balancing your psychological emotions, thinking, keeping cool and calm all the time, focussing on a positive attitude, helping each other to grow, compassion, empathy for others, doing regular work out, and yoga. Meditation to keep stable your thoughts and emotions will help you to grow both physically and mentally.

Health: Two aspects of physical and mental well being is the true **first pillars** of the wealth creation principle

Wealth: To run daily needs of life routine activities like food, shelter, and education you would need money to take care of basic needs for yourself and your family. One cannot eat and sleep peacefully if running a lot of loans or debts. So it is better to have at least, 3- 6 months of your wealth saved to take care of in case of an emergency both for you and unexpected family needs.

Family & happiness: 3rd Pillar of life and system built to support you in all aspects. You will feel more happy, joyous, and peaceful when at home along with your kids, parents, spouse, brother, and sisters. They will be there to support you in different situations like happy as well as sad or difficult. So are you. If one of your family members is sick, you feel worried, and that thought process will be always running in the back of the head until he gets well.

If you are not happy or not doing something you love or are passionate about, I am pretty sure you will quit in a while

Happiness is another key ingredient you have to have, whatever you do over the long term. If you love what you do, it feels like you working very hard for others but feels like a play for you. You won't get tired because you are interested and love your work.

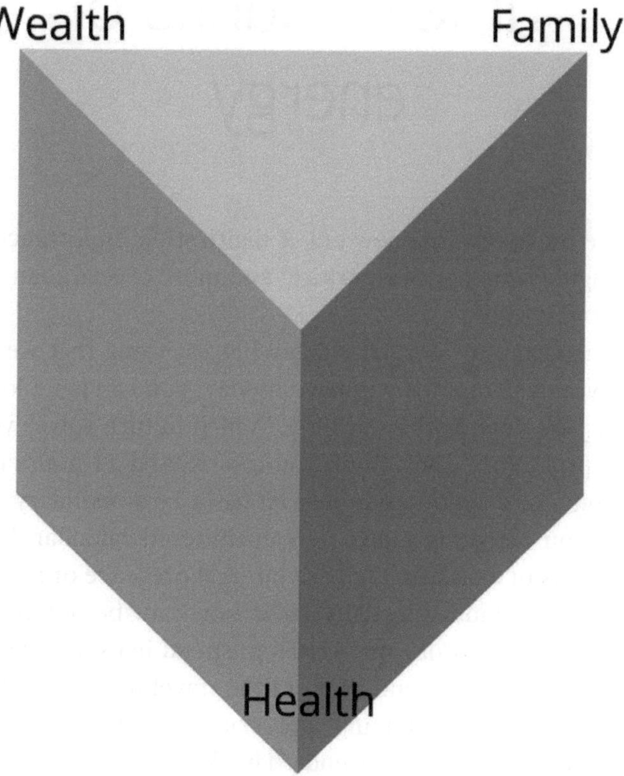

Pillars of Wealth creation

CHAPTER THREE

Time - chunks of energy

As we move towards new era of digitization importance of managing time has been critical and more crucial than any other part of life.

According to Morgan Stanley biggest thing that wealth gets you is “Time”. If you have money, you can get a lot of labor jobs done within no time. Which in turn solves your time problem. I don’t think you can expand 24 hours into 25 hours or even by a minute as it has a hard boundary. But what you can do is adjust your uncluttered calendar. Meet the needs of a task that needs your real presence or not.

A lot of mundane daily tasks now can be automated which saves a lot of time. I used to spend ina sane amount of time. I used to spend a lot of time traveling to the office, during weekends buying groceries, vegetables, fruits, shopping, and meeting friends. Thanks to covid luckily the other thing it thought is digitization. Any work, the business you can do at your fingertips.

Due to covid work from home provided and saved 4-5 hours of travel time thrice a week, averaging 15-20 hours. Shopping for groceries, fruits, and veggies in a crowded place line Bangalore would save 4 hours over a weekend.

Paying bills, mobile, utility, etc would save another 2 hours and a round trip to these offices save 2 hours with fuel cost savings and energy of mine.

So this in the same amount of time saved me my energy which is invaluable time and cost of fuel in turn this is being utilized for creating something beneficial useful either for myself or society.

Time Chart Savings

Before	After
20 hours of trave to office	Used 20 hours in learning new skill , reading and writing
5 hours of shopping groceries	Ulsed in building blog site
2 hours spent on utility payments	Used in learning new hobby

Time chart Savings - Sample example

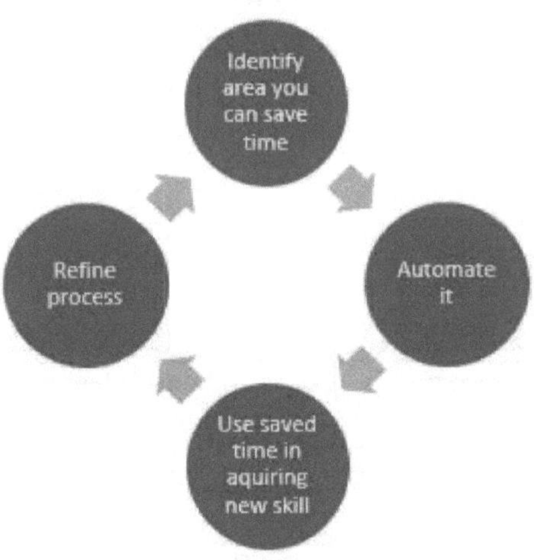

Save Time Process

CHAPTER FOUR

Building value system

Whether you are a technology geek, creative artist, writer, blogger, or industrialist if you have not produced a system of value that makes other people's jobs easy, if your article is not creating some value or information, then no one is going to buy it or value it.

Wealth derived out of your system should be organic. Based on a true, genuine product or service. Let me give an example in the real world. Lots of financial advisors, insurance agents, fool people in the name of policies, get rich quick schemes in getting customers' hard-earned money in trouble. Without exposing the risks, loopholes, and drawbacks, genuine money earned would be lost. The only motive behind these agents is getting rich by adding people into schemes through "Commission" making other people fool.

Another example of the same at a multitude of collapsing one's wealth is fintech apps. Most the apps allow buying shares of the company without giving the customer any clue of what is happening behind the scene,

A lot of times the customer may be aware of the share is going down without knowledge of why it is going down.

It may be macroeconomics like a war happening, a country in long-term debt, or due to political crisis which brings the overall market down. Sometimes due to microeconomics like a company filing bankruptcy or resolving insolvency issues they sell the company.

At least in my experience what I have known very fewer apps like Zerodha has a nudge feature that warns investor while buying any such risky assets.

Value systems in business are based on this principle which will have enormous growth opportunities and give real value to end-users. It also protects the investor's wealth at all times.

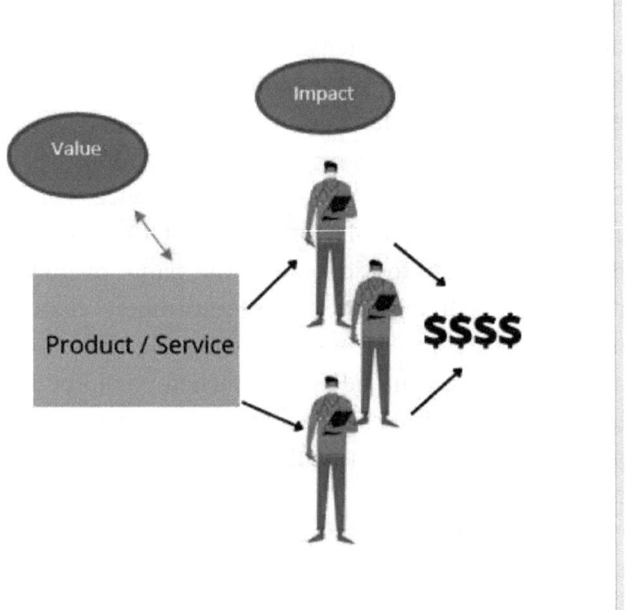

Build Value System

CHAPTER FIVE

Modern Wealth Creation Machines

As one of the famous entrepreneurs and famous people Naval Ravikanth said, you will not be able to get super-rich or even rich by renting out time. Even if you are in a specialty occupation like doctor or engineer or lawyer. For you to get rich you to have work, that would be not true when you having a holiday or sleeping or you fell sick.

In the early days, people made businesses like core industries which had land-made real estate businesses, and who had business from a family background like oil, mines, groceries, cloth industry. But that is not the case now, people with zero capital but only the notion of knowledge and creativity build multi-crore businesses.

A new trend in the digital era has already begun.

Facebook founder Mark Zuckerberg built a billion-dollar business using Facebook, Starting with a small social media sharing platform, Facebook grew as the biggest whale in the blue ocean. So in the case of Microsoft, Amazon, and apple some creative ideas behind founders lead to generating a money-making tree.

Softwares, technology platforms digital apps created in corner offices work round the clock without getting tired or without any intervention from a middle man.

They can be scaled to smaller groups, cities, country world. There is no limit. Practically it can grow infinitely big.

Similarly, media in the new era have reached to next level for users to give information. At the fingertips and fraction of a second, updated news is available to users.

Lots of new aged media companies like CNN, BBC, and Quint have generated crores of revenue through quality news content. They also generate a lot of revenue through ads and marketing.

Unless you own a business that is profit-making or are invested in a business that grows year on year consistently you have the potential to create a business and the know-how to sell, you are not going to be super-wealthy. Compounding works great not only in equity but also in good businesses.

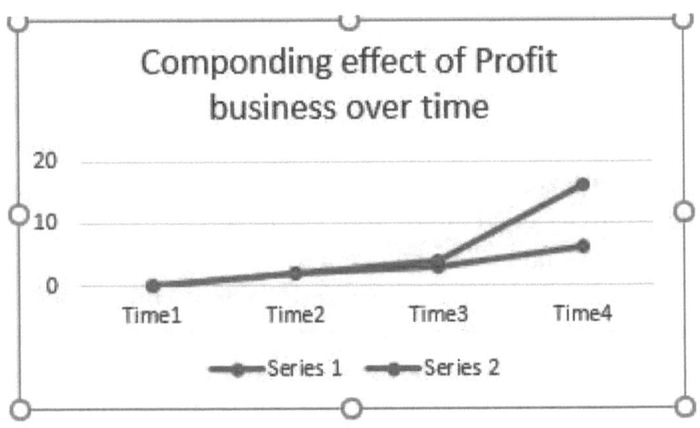

Compounding effect

CHAPTER SIX

Leverage strategy

If you want to succeed before spending lots of amount of dollars on setting up a team, infrastructure, marketing, and any additional cost associated or getting yourself drowned in debt are first to try out if your idea is getting working out. To do so share with people, ask them to try, review, try to improvise the product.

If people are ready to buy your product, or service at even 50% less than the cost of a competitor, then it will probably survive in the market. the

If you are impacting millions of people with a core of your philosophy and that is making it a little less complex than it was, the probability of succeeding is more. If you can build a trust system, a belief system to leverage both capitals, then that would be a great start.

If you think, you need a lot of capital and labor-intensive business that needs to be leveraged, that works through this system.

You have to build a system of trust, success with low-cost proves the probability of succeeding is more, then people will leverage you with what you need.

Labour and the working class need a direction in which they should burn their time and energy. Captial needs to sit on the right seat before it starts compounding effect.

To Einstein's famous theory of relativity E = MC^2, meaning energy is a product of mass multiplied by the speed of light squared. In this equation, he explained, how energy is derived.

Similarly, Wealth = Capital * Labour ^2

Where,

Capital spent & Resources working time of Labour

The more expansion, the more labor, and more business. For example, if you look at some large organizations like TCS, and Infosys they add approximately 50K to 1 Lakh labor each year to expand growth and profit.

Leverage Strategy

There could be few exceptions to this, modern startups can be built nearing zero cost and automated infrastructure. I presume even in their minimal amount of capital and labor leverage is required is starting.

CHAPTER SEVEN

Experiment side projects

No human being on earth has become insanely rich overnight. You should have love, passion, and a vision of achieving something. Hard work is needed but smart work is more important. Try and experiment with each of your idea or your passion at least for 30 days to prove to yourself that your idea will stay longer in your head.

The human brain is a wonderful piece of creativity. It will be your day job. But parallel you can work on taking up small projects like blogging, learning, new technologies, teaching, youtube videos, and sharing creative content on social media will boost your potential.

Nowadays through youtube videos and creativity only a lot of new-age youth have built and earning in millions. Example Ali Abdal, UK-based medical practitioner. He has a habit of reading, blogging, youtube creative videos, and teaching. A lot of people;e started following and also started monetizing his channel. Over some time he became a millionaire.

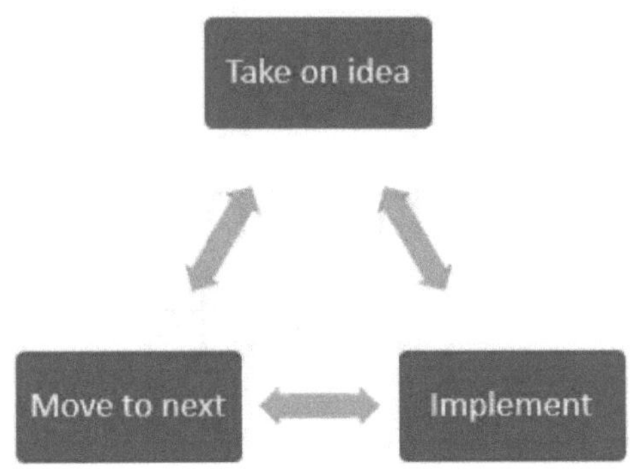

Side Project execution

CHAPTER EIGHT

Creativity - Heart of Everything

Creativity is the heart and soul of anything you do in life. If we don't think and look at creative art in each of our common routine activities life would become boring.

Look back and get amazed at some of the classic products like Apple touch screens, Windows operating systems, and the invention of Cars, founders behind had a creative mind.

This creative piece they visualized, thought about it, implemented, and scaled to market to reach millions then only that creative flew with flying colors.

How an artist creates art or a piece of wonder from anything, you can see an infinite number of ideas and possibilities to create wealth. The idea of infinite opportunities is paralyzing unless you pick up very few and implement them to generate revenue.

Society will reward creativity. If the problem-solving skill is artistic. Artistic I mean, that no one else could envision or solve that problem.

If everyone would not visualize, you have visualized and solved means that is a piece of art. There is no upper bound value for art. Society can only utilize and reward as much as it can.

Artistic ability combined with technology or media can boost your wealth creation strategies infinite times.

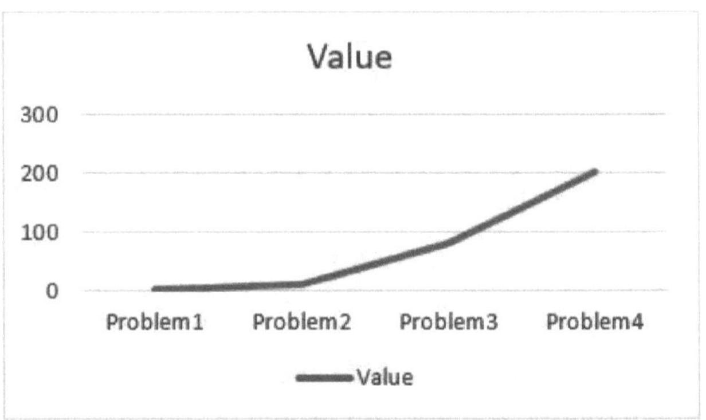

Value System

CHAPTER NINE

Reading - Notion of Wealth

A lot of times, we underestimate the power of reading, and writing skills for knowledge improvement and skill-building. An author of the book would have spent a lot of effort in visualizing his ideas, putting them into words, and making a collection of his life experiences skill into a book.

Great leaders, entrepreneurs, and creators have this habit of reading. There is no other equivalent to reading. Because from my experience, reading imprints the ideas that the author has envisioned straight into your mind.

Even though in the modern era, there are new ways of information sharing through various platforms like social media, Facebook, Instagram, linked in, youtube, audiobooks, ebooks from my experience, I feel the traditional way of reading paperback version with hardcover, I feel the most effective one.

There are also a few reasons like how our brain is wired for many many years. What we hold physically through our hands, our legs, what we feel, the smell of a book, the color of the book in the real, artistic design of the book. These small chunks set the ambiance of a long-lasting effect on your brain.

Experiment with taking 2 different books of your choice. One with paperback and another with the audiobook version of the book. Try reading and listening, make notes if you wish. Then leave it for a while, let's say 3 months.

After 3 months, make a note of what you remember from both books, and write it down. You would realize what I said !!!

So the abundance of knowledge, skill, and philosophies once get imprinted in your brain, I am sure, even if the wealth is lost whatever you have earned, can be created in a matter of a year or two.

Here we are talking about the wealth of knowledge that no one can steal and which is in my opinion true notion of wealth behind any business or person so to speak !!

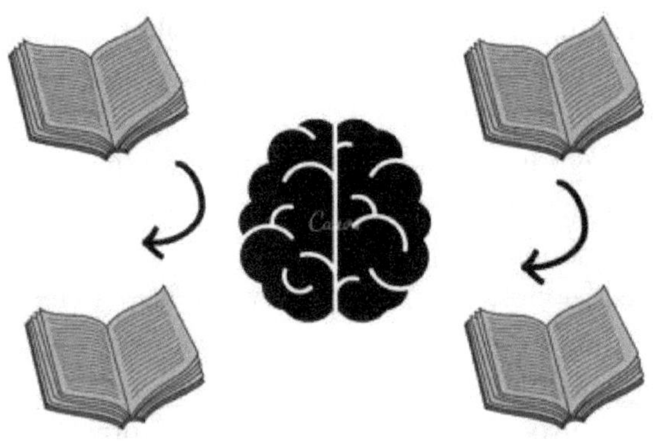

Knowledge building Strategy

CHAPTER TEN

Summary

If you are reading until here, means you have reached the end of the book. I am sure you have loved the wealth creation strategies explained in this book.

We started with Philosophy, Pillars, and the importance of time. Also, we discovered what a value system means and how you can build a credible wealth creation engine using a leverage strategy. Keep in mind side projects are also important, along with creativity and knowledge inputs.

Thanks for taking the time to read and enjoy the journey of wealth creation !!!

Printed by Libri Plureos GmbH in Hamburg, Germany